This book belongs to:

____

ALL OF THE MANY PATTERNS

For information contact:
camelscrafts@gmail.com
Written and illustrated by Camille Worsham
Published in Orem, UT, USA
First Edition
ISBN: 978-1-7369022-0-2
Library of Congress Control Number: 2021905793
Printed in the United States of America
First Edition: April 2021

ALL OF THE MANY PATTERNS

Written and Illustrated by CAMILLE WORSHAM

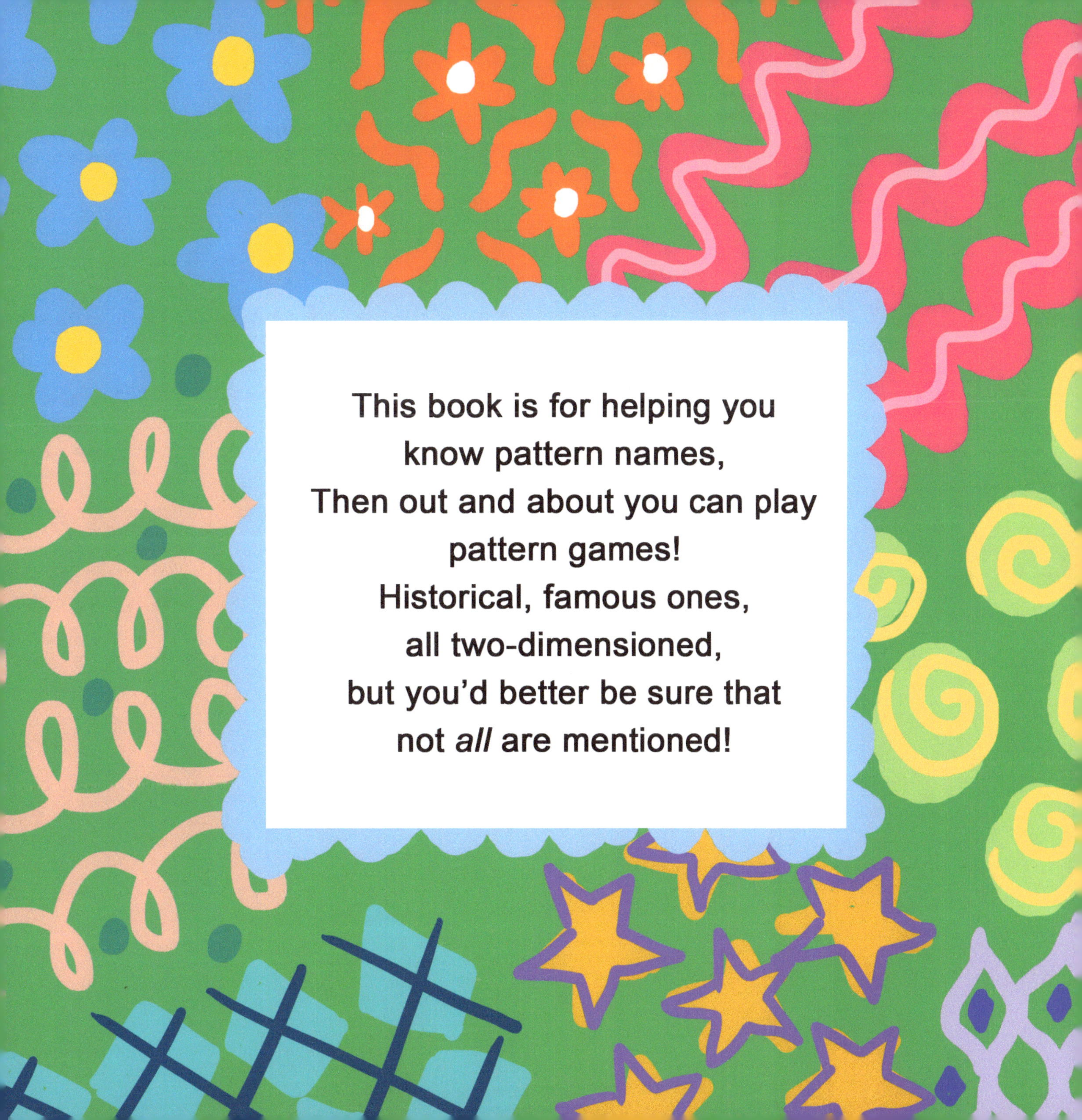
This book is for helping you
know pattern names,
Then out and about you can play
pattern games!
Historical, famous ones,
all two-dimensioned,
but you'd better be sure that
not *all* are mentioned!

How
Americana!

These teardrop shapes here
make a pattern called "Paisleys",

They sometimes have flowers
and sometimes have crazies,

Their fish-shapes are kinda
like little bananas,

You'll find paisley
patterns on cowboy
bandanas.

This one is common!
"Florals" have flowers!

They're fancy or simple
(like ones that have powers)

They come in all colors with pieces
botannical,

With blossoms, and leaves, and towers of
pannicle

Geometric patterns have many many types.

Just don't get me started on all of the stripes!

They've got zig zags, and chevrons, and some polka dots.

Or squares, and circles, and sometimes some blots.

- monkey
- frisbee
- chandelier
- squirrel
- tire swing
- two books
- lion's face
- diving duck
- soccer ball
- turtle
- unattended backpack

This one from Jouy is a pattern called "Toile",

It's made up of scenes. Can you find them all?

When lines cross like this, the
pattern's called plaid,
Or gingham or tartan,
(They all are just rad).

We wear them a lot,
like on the farm.
The colors are layered,
it's part of the charm.

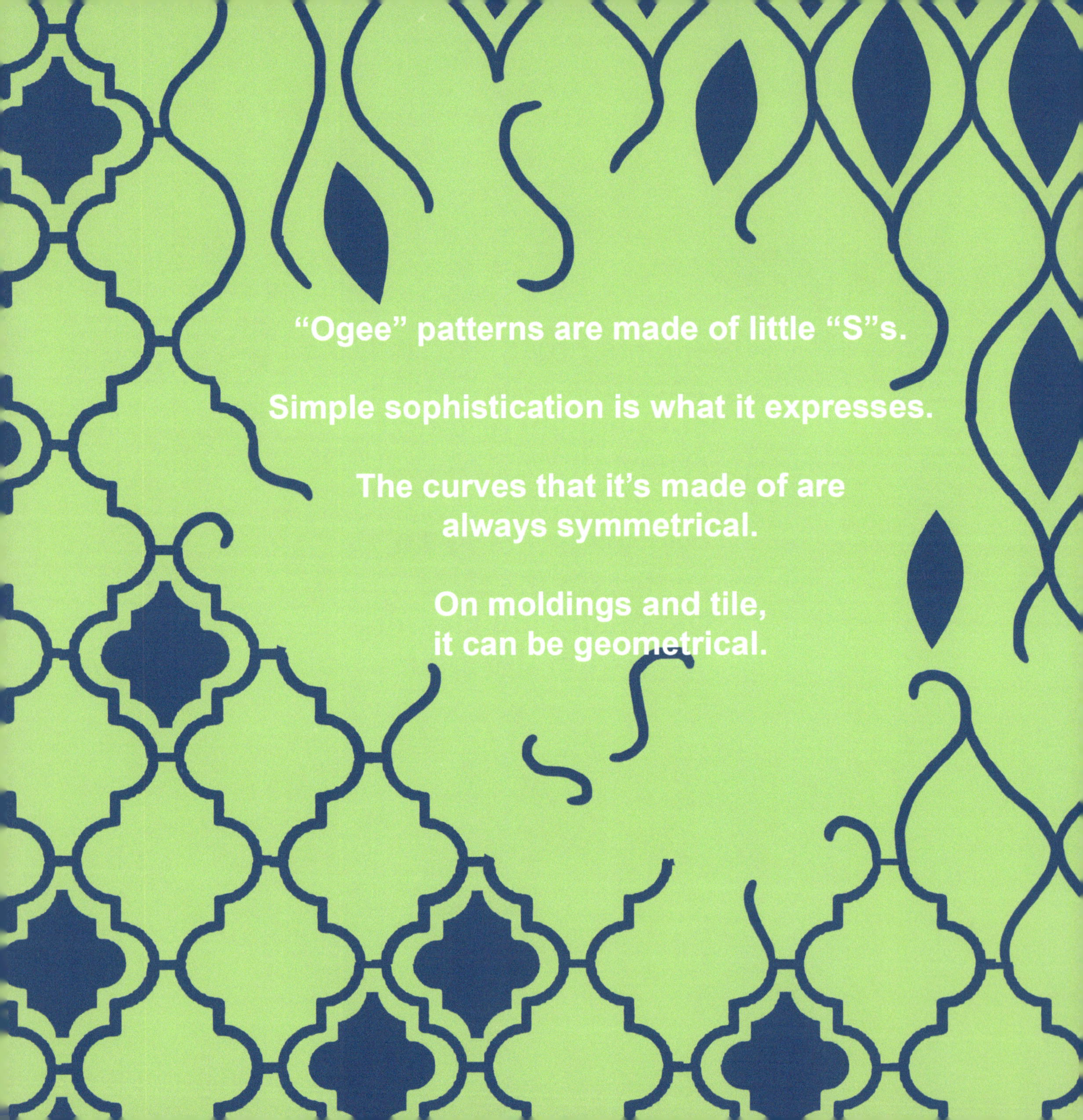

"Ogee" patterns are made of little "S"s.

Simple sophistication is what it expresses.

The curves that it's made of are
always symmetrical.

On moldings and tile,
it can be geometrical.

"Herringbone"'s named from the
Herring fish bone,
When you weave a twill,
it's the threads that are shown.

They make this one on the floor with tile,
Like a chevron, it repeats
for quite some while.

This one is called "Damask".
Can't you just *feel* the drama?

It's in diamond formation, worn
by the king's momma.

"Checkered"s a pattern
on games, flags, and
floors.

It's usually greyscale to
set off the scores.

When it's diamonds instead
it's called "Harlequin".

The court jester thinks that
the style's very *in*.

"Houndstooth" is interesting
as you can see.

All of the pieces fit perfectly!

The pattern is ancient,
it comes from it's weaving.

With pop culture references,
Houndstooth ain't leaving.

"Chinoiserie" is fancy
with monkeys and things.

They're elegant patterns,
with plants and bird wings.

This pattern first came all the way
from far Asia.

It's delicate, pastel,
and sure is fantasia.

Now "Animal Print" patterns
are different from the rest,
In the fashion industry they're
one of the best.

They look like the skin
of a camouflaged beast.
It's a controversial thing,
the way they are pieced.

nature

Patterns are great with all their tessellations,
And now you can name them in all situations!

Whether math, or in nature, or just decorations,
Patterns are welcome in all our creations!

math

PRONUNCIATION GUIDE

Chinoiserie (sheen-WAH-zer-ee) A pattern, usually from the 18th century, that imitates Chinese motifs in Western art

Damask (DAM-isk) A reversible woven fabric

Harlequin (HAR-luh-kwin) A diamond shaped pattern

Jouy (JOO-ee) The shortened version of the french town where the "Toile de Jouy" pattern was first produced

Ogee (OH-jee) a symmetrical S-shaped curve

Toile (Twall) from "Toile de Jouy", a pattern of pastoral scenes printed in one color, usually on a white or cream base

www.ingramcontent.com/pod-product-compliance
Lightning Source LLC
Chambersburg PA
CBHW042134030726
47599CB00002B/467